T0147875

JESUS
cast them devils out

JESUS
cast them devils out

CHRISTINA V. ESPINOSA

iUniverse, Inc.
Bloomington

JESUS cast them devils out

iUniverse books may be ordered through booksellers or by contacting:

iUniverse
1663 Liberty Drive
Bloomington, IN 47403
www.iuniverse.com
1-800-Authors (1-800-288-4677)

Copyright © 2009, 2011 by Christina V. Espinosa.
T.F.G. Ministries
P.O. Box 14323
San Antonio, TX 78214

ISBN: 978-1-4620-5979-9 (sc)
ISBN: 978-1-4620-5980-5 (ebk)

Printed in the United States of America
iUniverse rev. date: 10/13/2011

TABLE OF CONTENTS

INTRODUCTION

ᴊESUS, I LOVE YOU SO much for showing your mercy and saving my soul from damnation. Jesus let this testimony you have given me reach out to millions of souls and be delivered into your heavenly kingdom. My name is not important, but the message is. I didn't truly believe there was a devil and God, but the series of event has caused me to change my way of thinking and hope it changes yours too, and if you're not saved, TAKE A CHANCE AND DON'T WAIT 4EVER, because you don't know what tomorrow brings. Repent FOR THE END IS NEAR.

MY CHILDHOOD EXPERIENCES

I REMEMBER GOING TO SHERATON BAPTIST Church on Sunday mornings on the bus. There were classes, scripture contest and picnics. We learned about Jesus coming into our heart and I felt I had him in my heart. My grandma used to take me to her church at St. Joseph's church. We would sing and do communion, but I remember that I was never asked to accept Jesus into my heart, but I still went. I went to another church that was the First Assembly of God and I felt like it was more appealing to my soul. I remember singing praises to the Lord and hearing teachings from the Bible. The Church taught about salvation and changing my life for Jesus. We watched a film about the Mark of the Beast and this church is where I saw a demon possessed person for the first time. It scared me so much because I was only 12 years old.

I was always in church from the ages four to sixteen and that's when I stopped going. I started to have a dream over and over. I would wake up and feel something pulling me and it had sharp claws. I would try to scream and my mouth would open, but no noise would come out. I remember this thing would grab my leg and scratch me. I finally would get away and run to my door, and the door would close. Everything in the room would start to shake. I would manage to get the door open, and my grandma would be grabbing my right hand, and this thing would be grabbing my left hand and then I would wake up. This dream happened so much that I was afraid to go in my closet because that's where that thing would come out. I would check to see if there was any blood or scratches but nothing.

I never knew what this dream was about until now. It was a fight for my soul. At the age of sixteen, I went to a retreat with my grandma, and this Pastor came up to me and told me about my brother losing his hair. I was shocked that he knew about my brother. He told me that it was evilness around him and told me to tell him to get right with God, and have faith, and his hair would grow back. I returned back home and told my mother and brother about what the Pastor had told me. My mother tried so many treatments including going to Mexico dealing with the witch doctors. She didn't know any better. We were all lost and needed to find Jesus.

My family grew up in drinking, fighting, and drugs. I remember trying to smoke cigarettes, and my grandma caught me and made me eat them. It sure worked because I didn't touch them again until I was in my thirties. I had painful memories of being molested by three different guys. Mothers out there know who your child is staying with and who comes over! I am so glad my mother believed me and not like some mothers/parents who blame their daughter or son for what happened. I started to drink with my brothers and cousins and then came the weed. I got so drunk with my brother at his friend's house, and went to lie down and dozed off, and woke up to a man on top of me raping me and I was helpless. I pray for all the young girls/women that this never happens. Don't let yourself be put in this position ever. If I'd known Jesus I wouldn't have been polluting his temple with alcohol.

POLLUTING GOD'S TEMPLE

In June 1986, I graduated from High School and soon after I enlisted in the Army. My first station was in Stuttgart Germany. It seemed the Military liked to party. I would go downtown drinking all night coming back one hour before work and taking a shower and going to work at 6 am. This went on so long. Some events had occurred while at my first station which were rape, sexual harassment, and becoming a single parent, which caused my company commander to assign me to another company. The father of my child was happy about the baby. He told me he would be there. It was the complete opposite; he denied he was the father. I was enraged; how could he lie? I was going to do everything in my power to have the courts acknowledge him as the father. He refused to even take a blood test that the military made him do and he was found the father of my daughter. I was ready to move to another station and the lawyers set an amount for him to pay, but my leaving Germany messed things up. My daughter has never seen her father and he has never paid any child support. I keep thinking if I'd follow the ways of a Christian, I would've waited until God put someone in my path, got married and then have children. My next duty station was Honolulu Hawaii where I stayed for thirteen years of sinning, polluting my temple.

VOICES AROUND ME/DEMONS TALKING & TOUCHING ME ARE THEY IN ME OR AROUND ME

WAS IN HAWAII AND I loved it. I still continued to drink heavily and go clubbing with girlfriends I met at my station. I started to date but I just couldn't get over how I was treated over the years with men so I just could not get close to anyone, but I never went for the same sex. I started to feel revenge against men for what they did to me. I would go to these nice clubs where men would buy me a drink. They would be nicely dressed with diamonds around their necks, fingers and wrists. I found out they were pimps, and some of my friends were involved in this life style. I grew up poor, and was interested in finding how I could get money. I learned from my girlfriends and tried it my way without a man and was making lots of money until girls on the track would get mad and their man would chase me and beat me and told me I needed a man to work out there. I did get with a man and didn't like the idea of giving him my money so I would stuff money before he could even find out. I already didn't like men for what they did to me. I definitely wasn't going for that. I would see all these girls getting beat up, burned and some even branded. While on the streets, I would hear horror stories these girls went through and I only had a few but not as terrible as them like having a gun put to their head, or a knife at their throat, or locked in a room beaten and stabbed for days being raped over and over with a stick. I didn't stay with a man for long because I wanted my freedom, so I would come out early, get money, and be home for the night or go clubbing.

In Hawaii, most of the girls went for the Japanese because they were filthy rich and I wasn't wasting my time with little money; I was going for the gusto. I started to pick pockets, go into safes, and con men into thinking they were going to have the time of their life. I look back and see that I was doing the devil's work where he comes to kill, steal and destroy. I became one of the best thieves and stole millions of dollars and it went to waste. I wasn't considered a prostitute but many called me "The Thief". I could remember after stealing from these men an inner voice saying "Why did you do that? It is wrong" and suddenly another voice would say "They deserved it. They shouldn't be cheating on their wife. That's what they get." I had nine cars and jewels from the neck down to the ankle, but one thing I didn't have was Jesus in my life.

I was by myself for a long time and then I met a man who was a cook. I liked him from the start because he was not a pimp. He seem very nice and introduced me to cocaine, which I liked and kept doing it. I fell in love with him so much and started to get a thought that he was messing around. I kept getting that thought so I went over to see if he was and listened at the door and sure enough there was a woman there. I started to cry and pound on the door and he told me to go away. I told myself I would never talk to him. He would come with his smooth talking voice and I would accept him back. I started to hear voices while in his room and this is before I started doing cocaine. I would hear him talking and look at him, and his lips wouldn't be moving. I wouldn't think anything of it just thought I was hearing things. I started to do coke with him but he told me he liked ice. I had never tried it, but he told me it was a cool high and I would like it. I tried it and to this day I don't know what happened but it was so scary. Some of you might think this is a laughing matter but it's not. I could've been killed for what actions I did for the fear of my life. I was so scared knowing I was not alone in the unseen. I thanked the Lord. He had his hand upon me. I tried ice for the first time with Keith and he had to leave for work in the afternoon so I was left alone and that's when I was scared for my life. I started to hear all these voices and would look at people and their lips wouldn't be moving so I wondered who was talking. I got in my car and started speeding on the streets hearing voices that they were going to catch me and shoot me in the head. I would see a car coming up to me and hear them saying they were going to kill me so I would do a u-turn in the middle of the street, and jumped on a highway and sped so fast running red lights fearing for my life. I parked at a hotel and thought I was safe but no they were still out to get me. I got so tired and put my head down on the steering wheel and could hear many feet running towards me and then I would look up and nothing would be there. I finally got to see them and they were black figures with no eyes and they were talking to me. I told them I would get out. I got out and these black figures ran towards me and sat me down on the sidewalk scanning my body with this machine. I would try to look at them and they would disappear. They were talking to me. I didn't know who they were. I thought they were the FBI. They scanned my body so many times that I feel asleep. I woke up and my back was hurting and they had some hot machine going over my top left back over and over. It felt like something was done to my back. I remember this machine that scanned my body showed an x-ray of my insides. These figures came and they have grass skirts on and a long metal pole with feathers and some metallic wires on it. They would brush this all over my body. I was on the ground all night long. It was morning. These figures were under the ground. I saw their heads poking out of the ground talking to me. People would be coming out of a house and ask me "Is everything alright?" and I would reply "I'm okay". These two heads in the ground would be leaving and running to a place they needed to be. I could hear the sound of them running and when I would try to look at them they would stick their heads in the ground. I continued to see them leave until it

because the church has you in prayer. At the airport I could still hear these voices and they would tell me "You can't run from us; we will always be with you." I believe the Lord put me through three situations being put in the stage of killing yourself, put in a mental hospital to drug the demon, and being delivered and saved by the Lord.

I arrived in San Antonio, Texas where these voices followed me. The three categories were the first one I was driving and these voices were loud and she said "She's going to kill herself and another said if she does we'll take it out of her," but again God had his hand upon me. The second situation was these voices were making me scared so I kept a knife with me. My mom was concerned that she took me to go to a mental hospital. I walked in and I heard more voices than the ones I was hearing. I became so frightened because I heard a staff say "We'll drug her up and that's the end of that problem. It was taking so long that I left. I felt they were going to drug me and make me crazy. My mom was mad at me, but after talking to preachers she knew what was going on, and was glad I never stayed. The third is delivered and saved of the Lord. I look back what I went through and say "God must've known I could handle this because he doesn't put us through something we can't handle. The Lord revealed to me these people that hear and see things know what's going on. I myself went through these and I believe I went through them so I could help those being tormented like I was. The rest of you that call me crazy perhaps you don't know we're not alone and if you don't have JESUS in your life, its time to take action now!! Pray!! God wants our soul to be delivered, but the devil also wants our soul to devour it!! Where's your soul going? I was in Texas where my mom asked me to go to church and I would make so many excuses, then finally I gave in to make her happy. These voices went to church with me. I continued to party and these voices would be commenting on the sins I was doing. They told me about the music I listened too, and said I got good taste. They talked about the men I was seeing. As I was doing drugs I would here two voices discussing if I was going to overdose or what. I still didn't know who they were. I stated earlier I thought they were the FBI.

I continued in my daily life with these voices wherever I was. One night I was being tormented by them. They were saying things like "Here we come," and I could hear them running towards the door. I asked them, "How do you know me?" and they replied, "We always knew you; and I said, "Who are you?" A man's voice said we're the FBI and I said "you're lying; no you're not; who are you? A man's voice replied "We're the devil's association and another voice said you told her. I was shocked to hear that. I was brought up in a church knew of God but didn't really know who God was and wanted to know who this God was because I feared for my life.

In January 2003 I received Christ in my heart, but not fully with him. I continued to sin and go to church. The devil kept telling me, "Why are you going to church? You're still sinning anyways, but I still kept going. These voices were as clear as they were in the same room as me. I struggled in my walk with Christ. Day by day night by night I was being tormented so much. My mom had preachers pray for me, but the voices remained and tormenting too. I felt I was going crazy and wanted to take my life. I didn't know what to do. I needed to get closer to Christ so I prayed and prayed and prayed.

WALK WITH CHRIST

OMETIME IN THE MIDDLE OF April 2003, I was on the couch praying to the Lord, telling him to come into my heart, change me; I don't want to sin no more. Please help me . . . Suddenly tears came down and kept coming down. I felt peace all around me. I was delivered from drugs! Thank-you JESUS . . . The next morning I usually watch TV shows all day and night, but I didn't care for it. I picked up a Bible and started to read it. I wanted to know everything about JESUS and soon started to learn scriptures for defeating the enemy. These voices would be saying "She's reading the Bible, and she's learning scriptures. She's getting stronger in the Lord." I just kept putting my time into the Lord. I started to have many dreams, and I wasn't watching TV. Some of the dreams I had were spiritually cleaning of my house, scriptures are the sword, defeating the enemy, repent for the end is near, letting me know that I still had opening I needed to shut, fighting evil spirits with a sword. I had a dream about I was in my house and all these demon were in the house and I started to say

JESUS and they were bowing every time I said it and they kept coming at me and suddenly I called out to God and he said leave her alone and then these demons started to leave. I would have dreams about praying for someone and the demon would come out and say "You're not Christ." And I would reply "Christ liveth in me." And this demon would flee. I had about 33 dreams in all. I continued to read the Bible and try to learn everything about JESUS. While in bed I could not sleep all night. I was being tormented so much. These voices were saying cruel things to me. I was up the whole night just being terrified. I started to say these scriptures to get rid of them. They wouldn't go away. I kept saying these scriptures. They still were tormenting me. I was so afraid. I believe the Lord heard my cry and spoke to me. The voice was a calm still voice, I felt peace and I was safe. He told me to continue learning scriptures and speak in tongues because the devil can't understand. He spoke of the spirits that were in the house and there were 13 and I brought 3 with me. They were the music, drug and Egypt spirit. He spoke of the people that were in this house before me. He told me to show my love for JESUS to bring others to Christ and stay strong. He said the Lord is going to use me. I kept reading the Bible and learning scriptures.

I started to spiritually clean my house getting rid of worldly music, clothes, pictures, idols and some of my children's toys. I wanted everything out not of God. As I was growing in CHRIST he began to tell me go pray for that person; me being a babe in CHRIST sometimes would do it and sometimes not. I wasn't used of going up to a complete stranger and asking them if I could pray for them. I prayed to the Lord to give me boldness so I wouldn't be afraid. It took some time, but the Lord was still working with me. When I would wake up I would be praying and asking the Lord to guide me through the day. Sometimes I started to talk to the Lord, because I needed that comfort. My children began to grow in CHRIST too. My daughter and I were at this church and we were singing songs of praise and a voice came to me and said "Someone's trying to go into your purse," and me not knowing the voice yet thinking it was the devil trying to distract me, so I asked the Lord if this is him please take care of the problem. I continued to sing when my daughter whispered, "Mom, someone's trying to go in your purse". I said "Don't worry". I kept praising the Lord and praying to him when my whole body began to shake and the Holy Spirit came upon me and those two boys stopped trying to get into my purse. I thanked the Lord so much for protecting me. I was learning of the voices. I wanted to hear of God's voice and cast out the other voices.

I still had some habits in my life. I couldn't believe how the Lord was talking to me. The devil kept saying "You're so bad; doing every sin, how is God going to use you? I battled with that a long time. God can use anybody he wants, no matter what was going on, or what you did. I knew in my heart that I'd had to stop everything.

In May the Lord delivered me from cigarettes. I didn't need any patches, gums or whatever the world had to offer. All it takes is the hand of God. I thank you

JESUS so much. I Love You. I still was drinking and I would hear the voice "No you have to stop. Don't do that." It wasn't long before I stopped with the help of JESUS. I stopped in the month of July 2003. In May 2004 it will be one year not smoking and in June 2004 there has been no alcohol of any kind going into the Lord's temple.

In August 2004 I was singing to Christian music when the Lord said, "sing the scriptures I put in your heart. I blessed you by putting my scriptures in your heart, so bless others by singing them wherever you go." I was shy to sing out loud because of my voice, but that was lies of that devil. He'll tell you anything just so you'll be too intimidated to speak out. People would laugh or look at me strange and that would make me say the scriptures even louder. The Lord would tell me to go up to that person and pray for him or tell him JESUS loves you, or whatever message He wanted me to say. As I mentioned I was shy and especially going up to a complete stranger. Of course that lying devil would be saying "They're going to laugh at you and call you crazy," and a whole bunch of lies. I had to tell that devil to shut up and in the name of JESUS get out of here. The Lord began to talk to me about having your feet ready to preach the Lord's word and give your testimony and said "Start with your neighbors. I said "Oh boy, I got to start with my neighbor. What will I say?" Use your pamphlets to begin a conversation. I didn't listen right away so a week goes by and the neighbor who never comes to me is in my face. Oh boy the Lord said "You're not going to go up to them so I brought them to you so tell them about me." I was talking about JESUS and introduced myself and asked them if they go to church and she said that she did go to church and I said you're welcome to go to my church if you like. Remember I was a babe in Christ, I should've asked her if she had JESUS in her heart.

The Lord began to speak to me everywhere, but sometimes I would listen and do what was instructed, but sometimes I was not obedient. I was still trying to learn and know the voice of the Lord. I would be asking, "Is this you, Lord?" I want to know. Please Lord; let me know how to tell your voice. People would tell me that his word would confirm with the Word of God. Oh Lord is this your will? Let me know. Many times these voices I would call upon the Lord and ask Is this you? I just wanted to learn about JESUS from hearing his voice, from reading the Bible, hearing sermons, spiritual books and talking to people who serve the Lord. We learned from each other and lift each other up when we were in need of help. I called unto the Lord. My first three months with Christ I was being tormented by the devil so much. I was so scared that I was talking to the Lord all through out the day. He was my true friend my refuge. I felt safe. He was right there with me through the valleys. He was with me in the fires, and the Lord can be with you whatever you're going through. Give your problems to him and ask him to help you. He loves us so much. He doesn't care what you did. Don't feel guilty, ashamed, and worthless or you're so bad the Lord will never help you. That's lies from the devil. JESUS wants his lost sheep to be found. He loved us so much that he died on the cross for all of us. Right now at the present time you're thinking what does she know. She doesn't know what I'm going through. You're absolutely right. I don't know but God knows. Give it to God and you'll see results. While I was reading the Bible, you see the signs and wonders he did in the past, but he still does it today . . . Call unto the Lord. Let him shelter you.

Once I was saved, I needed to root myself like praying, fasting, reading the Bible, memorizing scriptures, spiritually cleaning my house, fellowship with people in Christ, hearing sermons, reading spiritual books, disassociation from things and people in the past. I needed to get these habits out of my life, and the only way is seeking God all the days of my life. It's hard, but with God all things are possible. I made sure I wouldn't go places where I shouldn't. I'm not going to go to a bar, nightclub or dope house if I'm trying to change my ways for God. The devil knows what you used to do. He'll bring friends you haven't seen for ages to make you fall. He'll start to make you remember the times you were sinning and enjoying it. These are the thoughts and the thoughts turn into action. The devil is so mad because you belong in God's kingdom, so he's going to fight and use his traps to catch you slipping. A new babe in Christ has to root themselves, and call out to God for help. The devil uses everything he knows about you to make you fall. I learned scriptures and kept them in my heart so when temptations came I fought with the sword better known as scriptures. I was having hard time learning and understanding the bible to memorize them. These were lies from the devil. I did ask the Lord to help me

Let that devil know you are a child of God. The devil is not playing with you. He hates us because we're of God and he wants one thing our soul! Right now at the present moment who are you living for? People can tell by your daily living. Does you soul belong to God? Are you taking JESUS with you everywhere, and everyday asking him for guidance to give to you for that day? Are you going to church, hearing the word from the preacher? Are you studying the Bible? We have to make sure the preachers are preaching the truth of God. How do we know? We need to get into the Bible daily, seeking and asking JESUS to show us understanding and ask JESUS Is this true what the preacher said, Lord? Show me I feel so troubled. Are you one to read the Bible only on Sunday morning? How do you expect to get rooted? You sow what you reap. The devil will try to distract you when hearing the Word of God. You will begin to have thoughts enter your mind. CAST THEM OUT, if their not of God. The devil is stealing the word from you, and that's the word you need to hear. You must be in a quiet place and ask the Holy Spirit to come and open you up and get ready to receive. Try not to get distracted in all things. I listen to the sermon and mediate on what is being said. It's easy to be distracted when your eyes and mind are not on the Lord. Remember we need to renew our mind, for it is written we have the mind of Christ. What are you putting in your mind? Ungodly thoughts that the Lord hates or His word in your heart for keeps? Some of you don't even know if there is really a God or a devil? What are you going to do? Just let it go and hope it's not true, or seek the truth us. We all have stories that we want to put away secretly. There are things we are ashamed that might get out. We say "Oh No! What will they say when they find out? How will they treat me? Will they talk to me? Will they think less of me? Will they criticize me? Will they make me cry and hurt me inside?" All these questions went through my mind, but when the Lord put his hand upon me, I didn't care what people thought or said. The Lord had compassion on me. He knew everything I did and he forgave me. Some people will never accept me but if I know I serve a living God and if I do his will and obey his commandments and show my love for everyone on this earth, I will be rewarded. I will continue to love the Lord because he is so caring and merciful to forgive my wrong doings. I remember what I was into, and I thank the Lord so much for changing me. When I see someone in the same position I say "Lord that's where I was and you delivered me. Thank-you JESUS I love you so much. I know you can deliver them too." When I see someone crying or talking about problems I remember myself and tears start to come down. I pray for them to be delivered. No matter what you've done don't let the devil tell you God can't help you, because God knows what you're going through. He knows what you need, and he's ready to help. Just call him. JESUS JESUS I NEED YOU. HELP ME. PLEASE SAVE ME. DELIVER ME LORD, keep calling on Him until it happens. Don't give up keep calling Him. He knows your heart.

GOD'S WILL

YOU BELONG TO GOD'S KINGDOM since you made him Lord over your life. I have so much love for JESUS that I want to do his will. I want to be obedient to his spirit at all times. I want to stay so close to Him because He's my comforter. His will for us is his plan to be established. The main goal is help save the lost souls before it's too late. We might be put in the ministry or at the local gas station. We're all the same in God's eyes. Those well known are no more important than those not even known. The only thing matters are you serving God, doing his will? Or are you serving yourself and building kingdoms for yourself? God knows everyone's heart. People, who claim to be of God, may fool others but God is not mocked. He will allow things to glorify you and make you rich until He is angered and bring you down. If you're not doing God's will, get right with God and repent, before you're brought down. It's about doing God's will not your will. There is one God for the Bible tells us so. Look it up 1 Corinthians 8:5-6, and the devils also know, read James 2:19. The truth is shown, why do people have many gods? It's because satisfaction of the flesh. You ask yourself is this of God and then make excuses to accept them. There are so many gods to people like sports, money, sex, drugs, drinking, music, jewels, gambling, food, clothes, cars, prideful preachers and television. There's so many but let's stop here. I listed these because people sometimes glorify these things or people and not know it. The Holy Spirit will grieve and let you know when something is wrong. That is your new god if you continue to please the flesh or person instead of God. Do you love God? Or the devil? You can only serve one master. There are no in betweens.

Churches are scattered because of different beliefs. The belief is there is one God, so why are people praying to different gods? Why are people doing rituals? We ask the Lord to be in our life, baptized in His name, repent and we belong to his kingdoms. The truth is found in the Bible. People offer many ways to seek the Lord or get answered prayer by buying prayer cloths, pens, and ceramic angels. Let the truth be known and set those that are lost free. There is one way to get saved and that's through JESUS and only him. Watch out for those false prophets!!

HOLY SPIRIT

THE HOLY SPIRIT IS KNOWN as the comforter and the spirit of truth lives in me. He makes me feel safe knowing he'll protect me in time of trouble. He'll show me things to come. He'll teach me things I need to know or correct. He judges all things and lets me know what's not of God. He speaks of God not himself. The Holy Spirit is connected with God and me. I don't want to do anything to grieve Him, because I feel the conviction and the sadness of his voice when He's being grieved. He compares spiritual things with spiritual and teaches us not the words which man's wisdom teaches. He's always with me to comfort me. He's my friend, my true friend to the end. I talk to him always throughout the day. If a problem arises I ask him to help me. Oh, I'm so glad he's with me. What I was going through, my family thought I was crazy and wanted me to seek medical help. I got one thing to say if you are a believer and still struggle with addictions something is wrong. The Holy Spirit can deliver you from any stronghold. If there are still habits in your life after serving the Lord for many years, then there is a problem with your walk with Christ. There may be a door open, a curse brought upon you, a soul tie or words spoken against you. You need to break that stronghold and ask God for forgiveness.

These voices knew everything about my family's life. I kept saying, "Mom, how do they know everything? The voices replied" we always knew you and kept in contact all the time. I didn't know who these voices were but later I found out they were demons oppressing me. God knows why I went through this. I now understand why all these things happen to prepare me to help those in need.

All of you serving God can have a close relationship. It's up to you to seek him daily, and putting away the fleshy desires of this world. Those who don't even know about God need to find out the truth before it's too late. All of my youth life, I was in church until I strayed off. I knew of God, but didn't know truly about Him. I experienced these things that were so frightening and I was thinking about suicide. These voices were so loud. I wanted them to quit. I felt like I was going crazy. I called out to the Lord, Help me. Why am I going through this? All I know is God has His hand upon me and I love Him so much for bringing me through the fires. No matter what you're going through, God can help you! Call on him, and He will rescue you. Lord Jesus, I pray for those who are experiencing what I went through that they call out your name and be delivered. JESUS JESUS HELP ME I'M SO SCARED PROTECT ME LORD.

RENEWING OF THE MIND

I'M SAVED; NOW I NEED renewing of the mind because He's Lord of my life. The Lord started to clean me up internally and externally. I remember all these thoughts and voices going through my head. I had to put these things in to the right place. They either stayed in my heart or were casted out in the name of JESUS. We need to filter out our thoughts if they are of God. I felt at that time I needed to meditate on the word of God, and learn Scriptures and put them in my heart. I was a changed person when I accepted JESUS in my life. The happiness is all over me, the glow in my face. I believed we have renewed our mind when we speak the word of God always. We take JESUS wherever we go saying the scriptures in boldness or praising the Lord in singing songs or scriptures. I look back at my life what it used to be, how I used to speak. I'm always telling JESUS I love him so much because He changed me so much, and I don't care what I gave up because He was there when I needed Him. Conversations can be threatening if you don't know how to control your mind with the Word of God. You might have to hush up to ease the fire, but watch that devil; he will try to stir things up. The thoughts that come into your mind ask JESUS for filtering the good ones and bad ones. Renew your mind with the Word of God because the flesh lusts after the spirit.

SPIRITUAL GIFTS/FRUITS

READ THE BIBLE AND CAME across the Spiritual Gifts and asked myself "What are those? The Lord answered these are gifts that available to those who seek me diligently. I fell in love with JESUS and I wanted to know everything there was to know about Him and have a close relationship. I started to pray always and reading my Bible and asking the Lord for the understanding and for the Spiritual Gifts. I kept praying for the Gifts and asking JESUS what must I do. I want to know everything about Him. JESUS, you delivered me and saved me. There are gifts and fruits that JESUS will give us. I look at myself as an example. I started to read the Bible asking to memorize them and the Lord answered my prayer. Next I asked the Lord for understanding while reading the Bible, and little by little I started to understand. While I was singing a spiritual song on the radio the Lord said sing the scriptures I put in your heart. I blessed you with the word, so wherever you go bless others. I listened to what the Lord told me.

I felt the gifts and fruits were increasing as I showed my pressing to my Lord. Some of the Fruits and Gifts may take times, but I'm taking one day at a time with my sweet JESUS. In everyday life, certain situations happen to see how you would react. Watch out! If you're not careful and you don't know how the Lord would want to handle the situation, you might say "my feelings are hurt" or they're going to get it. The things we say could be blowing our gifts and fruits the Lord is trying to give us. The Spiritual Gifts are Wisdom, Knowledge, Faith, Healing, Miracles, Prophecy, Discerning, Diverse Tongues and Interpret Tongues. The fruits of the Spirit are Love, Joy, Peace, Longsuffering, Gentleness, Goodness, Faith, Meekness, and Temperance. Is Christ is your life? Are you growing in Christ? It's time to get right with Christ and run the race. Even those who haven't accepted Christ can start. Look at my life, all the things I did and went through. The Lord changed me and I will continue to seek Him daily.

How do you know if you have certain fruits? Let's take love for example. In my case, I fell in love with JESUS and loved everyone and wanted to tell everybody about JESUS and what He did for me. The Joy in my heart keeps me going just knowing that JESUS is with me. Bad things may happen, but if I keep my eyes on the LORD, He will see me through and deliver me. The peace He has put in my heart and mind had kept me not worrying, not fearing, no more tormenting and no more restless nights. The longsuffering were the voices and trials and tormenting that I was going through, but

God had his hand upon me. It was only for a season. Now when a problem arises I know the Lord will make a way to escape and He won't allow a problem that is too much for me to handle. The meekness is to humble myself. I find myself giving God all the glory no matter what it is.

Using the word I can open a door to the Pride spirit. I am careful not to give myself glory about anything. Those who glorify themselves shall be brought down. The gentleness and Goodness show how much heart you have towards people even your enemies. JESUS might tell you to do something for Him and you start to wonder. One thing is the devil is not going to like you being kind to one another. He's here to kill, steal, and destroy. People may take your kindness for weakness. Its sad how people are taken advantage when their asked to get a second mortgage on their home and being kept in debt while these preachers build kingdoms for themselves like million dollar homes, private jets, and extravagant vacations, high hotels cost per day. All these people follow these preachers and evangelists where ever they go coast to coast when they should be reading the word to get revelation from the Lord. Wake up! These false prophets are leading you to destruction. Prophecy is 100% correct not 99%, so if someone prophesizes something is going to happen in this year or whatever it may be if it doesn't happen that's a false prophet. Faith is to know that God has his hand upon you and no matter what you're going through He will be with you in the trials. Stay strong and have great faith in Him. If it's God's will it will be done. Patience for me is going to the store when someone runs into you and blames you or a slow person driving in front of you. Patience is a hard one for me, but God is molding me.

ARE YOU A HEARER AND A DOER?

Y WALK WITH CHRIST AND the leading of the Holy Spirit started to talk to me. He would show me my faults, directions and futuristic goals. I didn't know if this voice was from God or that lying devil. I started to ask God. Is this you? I would get an answer and sometimes I would have to wait. I was told to witness about JESUS to my neighbors, praying for someone, or tell somebody JESUS loves you. I wanted to tell everyone what JESUS did for me and how he delivered me. Sometimes I would catch myself being both a hearer and doer, but sometimes the devil would sneak in and start saying things "You don't even know these people; they're going to laugh at you; you got tomorrow because you have so many errands to do." I know now if it's not the fruits of the spirit, it's the devil. Tomorrow is not promised to you so I live day by day talking to the LORD. In the Bible it says the devil can be as an angel of light. That's why it's important to know God personally and follow the Holy Spirit's guidance. It could be preaching, teaching, spiritual music, but it's not God's doing. The way to seek God is talking to him directly and reading his word daily. You might find yourself watching Christian stations, listening to spiritual music, going to seminars, but you're neglecting your relationship with Jesus and not meditating on his word. In the Bible it says people will say "here is Jesus, come follow he is here in Jerusalem, even the elect shall be deceived." When I would be watching the Christian station the Holy Spirit will tell me, "what are you doing? Read your bible, talk to the lord".

ARE YOU PLEASING THE FLESH?

IN THE BIBLE THERE ARE 17 ungodly spirits that I believe are the main growth of the strongholds. If you take a look at all of these, after a while these spirits start to grow and destroy your soul internally. The body starts to go through problems sometimes leading to death. If you look at these spirits, they're all evil and are better if you stay away from them. The devil will let you have some power for a while, but when it's time for his payback he's taking one thing, your soul. Once these ungodly spirits manifest inside of you or your house they make it their home and start to bring other spirits to start their infestation. I was delivered. I didn't want any spirits of flesh in me or trying to come into me so I kept meditating on the word of God and saying Scriptures whenever a bad thought came into my mind. Don't ponder on evil thinking; that's how the spirit grows and gets stronger. Cast it out right away and ask Jesus to help control the thoughts with the word of God. Always meditate day and night, praying always and staying in the holy presence of God. Ask him to renew your mind because of that spiritual warfare going on. The 17 flesh spirits are Adultery, fornication, lasciviousness and uncleanness are the first ones listed. These are linked together. I believe that the lascivious spirit puts a thought in our head, making us desire fornication for anyone. It could be someone's husband, wife, brother, sister and the desire is so strong it could lead to adultery. After the sin's committed then the uncleanness spirit arrives and makes us feel unworthy. The rest are Idolatry, Witchcraft, Hatred, Variance, Emulations, Wrath, Strife, Seditions, Heresies, Envying, Murders, and Drunkenness. We need to walk in the spirit and not fulfill the lust of the flesh. These spirits are not of God. Ask the lord to help you if you are in battle with the spirits of the flesh. God can deliver you. Call out to God now. He's waiting for you.

SPIRITUAL BATTLEFIELD

WE ARE NOT FIGHTING WITH human flesh but of spirits around us or in people. It is very important to have the shield of Jesus to protect us. If we are not with Jesus, it gives the devil opportunities to throw his fury darts at you. Jesus died on the cross and provided a way for eternal life. He gave us the keys to bind and loose. Jesus gave us the keys to use, so let's use them. He also gave us the power to tread on serpents and scorpions and overall the power of the enemy. It is written nothing shall by any means hurt you. Everyday events happen in the news about people killing others, or themselves. It has nothing to do with the flesh but the spirit that overcame them. It is so important to filter our thoughts with the ways of God. That's why we need to read and understand the Bible. It's a way to live righteous in God's eyes. If you're trying to keep spirits from staying in your home you must control what's in your home, or who comes in your home. For it is written "first, say peace be to this house and then enter with god's shield". Always have and take Jesus with you, praying always and applying the blood. The devil always has tricks up his sleeves so be spiritually alert. Learn scriptures to defeat the enemy for it is written it is sharper than any two-edged sword. When I accepted Christ, I continued to pray, read, and talk to the lord daily about how to get rid of these strongholds. I must be connected to God and make sure I have all the doors closed to satan. Satan is ready to come into our lives and kill, steal, and destroy. The devil tries to enter many ways. The Lord will show you how to protect yourself. I can't stress enough you need to pray, read the bible and ask him for understanding. The devil enters into your dominion by sin, ancestry, transfer person to person, mind, music, movies, contact with the dead, emotional shocks, trauma, grief, bad habits, ungodly soul ties, unforgiveness, and the practice of cults. That is why we must protect our heart, soul, mind, and body. When we accept Jesus as our lord and savior, we must kill our flesh meaning not doing the desires of the flesh. We are changing our devilish ways into what God says we change our way of thinking by renewing of the mind with the scriptures engraved in our hearts. We are changing in what we used to do. God wants us to help lost souls be found. We want to serve God, being obedient to him, doing his will, and loving and praising him. When you love God you seek his word. You want to know all about him, and your heart desires moving closer to him in spirit and truth. All of these evil spirits are nothing when you know who you are in Christ Jesus and that you serve a living God.

died for me. Change me and send the comforter. You are the Lord of my life and I believe I am saved and will be baptized in your name. Here I am. Jesus, use me. Now when that person receives Jesus in their life, you must tell them how to root themselves. Tell them to pray to Jesus daily, talk to him as a friend, and read the bible, meditate to memorize scriptures. Ask them to find a church and Christian friends to fellowship and talk about the Lord or problems they're going through. Tell them the old friends you might have, have to go if they're not with God. Give them your number and tell them that they can call you if they have any problems. You continue to pray for that person to grow strong in the Lord. The shield of faith is protecting yourself and those the Lord has committed to you. Remember to apply the blood daily to yourself, family and friends to protect them. The devil can't touch you unless God says so. Just remember when your going through bad times, life threatening situations, bad habits, evilness surrounding you or deadly diseases, if you have faith the size of a mustard seed it shall be removed. I would say to God "Lord this trouble upon me, is this your will? If it's not take it away, or make a way for me to escape". Faith is to know you serve a living God and he has his hand upon you. No matter what problem arise; you know if your serving the Lord faithfully nothing shall by any means hurt you. Wear the helmet of salvation it's protecting your mind, your eyes, ears, and mouth. Whatever you do in everyday life, we must watch out what we see, do, hear, and think. We must have the mind of Christ with renewing of our mind. If we are doing ungodly things, it poisons our mind and grieves the Holy Spirit. We need to have the fruits of the spirit upon us daily even when we're so mad ready to scream and fight with somebody. We must go through trials and tribulations. Just have faith and hope that if you're serving a living God, He will be with you until the end. He will be with you in the fires, valleys, and the shadows of death if you let Him. Just remember the Lord is in control of your life and whatever battles you're going through, he will see you through. Just have hope in God, knowing his word for it is a sword you need. The sword is known as the Word of God. That's why we need to memorize scriptures when we are being tempted. I call the Word of God the unseen sword fighting against all evil that we do not see. The Lord had equipped us with everything we have to root ourselves. We do that by reading the Word of God, meditating, searching and living the way God wants us to. I once was mediating on Hebrews 4:12 and I fell asleep. The Lord showed me a dream. It consisted of evil spirits around me, and I would say Scriptures and a sword would be in my hand fighting with these spirits. One would die, and two others would come to fight and I would have to say these scriptures until it was over. That dream explained so much. We need to know the Word of God and memorize it and put in our heart. Some say it's so hard to memorize, but then the same people can know songs by heart. Don't be deceived by the devil letting him tell you it's so hard to memorize scriptures. He doesn't want you to learn them by heart, because that's his enemy. He knows once you know the word then he's got to go. Remember you need all these things to fight the spiritual warfare.

showing his love deeply. He also didn't condemn but said to save the unrighteous. God has equipped JESUS and JESUS equipped us and gave us everything he had. All we need to do is seek the Lord with all your heart, soul and mind. Do you want to know JESUS? You can begin a personal relationship with him now. Just seek SALVATION!!!

SALVATION IS NOW!

OW THAT YOU KNOW WHO JESUS is and what he did for you; what are you going to do? What kingdom do you want to belong to God's or satan's kingdom? Don't wait too long, because you don't know if tomorrow is promised to you.

What are you waiting for? Seek God's kingdom now!! JESUS is waiting for you with open arms. Call unto him.

JESUS, I need you. Forgive me of my sins.
Cleanse me with your blood.
Send me the comforter.
I want the Holy Spirit
I want to be baptized in your name.
JESUS Here I am. Use me.
I am yours forever; JESUS I love you
For having mercy on me.

You belong to God's kingdom, and the devil is mad at you. He will bring all evil forces to make you fall.

Root yourself in the Bible. Pray to the Lord and ask him to help you. Find a church to listen to the Word of God and find other believers that you can talk to about your walk with CHRIST. The one you should be talking to is JESUS. Start a personal relationship with Him. He will see you through the trials and tribulations. Stand fast and let's walk that narrow path together.

Well JESUS I love you and thank you for giving me this testimony. I hope this book helps many people and saves their souls.

Thanks JESUS
I LOVE YOU

MY FIRST SCRIPTURES
THE LORD GAVE ME

FIRST LEARNED THE PSALMS 23. I also learned about the name of Jesus, blood of Jesus, Word of God, praising Jesus, Defeating the enemy, Peaceful Mind, Holy Spirit, Keys to bind and loose, Ask and receive, Truth and Knowledge, healing, God's Love and Holiness, Forgiveness Scriptures. I know the Psalms 1-7, 91, 109, and 116 in my heart. I got delivered in April 2003 and started seeking the Lord. The Lord let me remember all these scriptures in 5 months. I couldn't believe it but I just kept taking in as much as I could. Here's my first Scriptures I learned.

Psalm 23

<u>The LORD [is] my shepherd; I shall not want.</u>

2 <u>He maketh me to lie down in green pastures: he leadeth me beside the still waters.</u>

3 <u>He restoreth my soul: he leadeth me in the paths of righteousness for his name's sake.</u>

4 Yea, though I walk through the valley of the shadow of death, I will fear no evil: for thou [art] with me; thy rod and thy staff they comfort me.

5 Thou preparest a table before me in the presence of mine enemies: thou anointest my head with oil; my cup runneth over.

6 Surely goodness and mercy shall follow me all the days of my life: and I will dwell in the house of the LORD for ever.

Name of JESUS

Philippians 2:10

10 That at the name of Jesus every knee should bow, of [things] in heaven, and [things] in earth, and [things] under the earth;

Proverbs 18:10

10 The name of the LORD [is] a strong tower: the righteous runneth into it, and is safe.

Matthew 1:21

21 And she shall bring forth a son, and thou shalt call his name JESUS: for he shall save his people from their sins.

Blood of JESUS

Hebrews 9:21

21 Moreover he sprinkled with blood both the tabernacle, and all the vessels of the ministry.

Matthew 26:28

²⁸ For this is my blood of the new testament, which is shed for many for the remission of sins.

Hebrews 9:22

²² And almost all things are by the law purged with blood; and without shedding of blood is no remission.

Word Of God

John 1:1

¹ In the beginning was the Word, and the Word was with God, and the Word was God.

Revelation 19:13

¹³ And he [was] clothed with a vesture dipped in blood: and his name is called The Word of God.

Ephesians 6:17

¹⁷ And take the helmet of salvation, and the sword of the Spirit, which is the word of God:

Praise the Lord

Psalm 135:1

¹ Praise ye the LORD. Praise ye the name of the LORD; praise [him], O ye servants of the LORD.

Psalm 18:49

⁴⁹ Therefore will I give thanks unto thee, O LORD, among the heathen, and sing praises unto thy name.

Psalm 115:18

¹⁸ But we will bless the LORD from this time forth and for evermore. Praise the LORD.

Psalm 100:4

⁴ Enter into his gates with thanksgiving, [and] into his courts with praise: be thankful unto him, [and] bless his name.

Peaceful Mind

2 Timothy 1:7

⁷ For God hath not given us the spirit of fear; but of power, and of love, and of a sound mind.

Philippians 4:7

⁷ And the peace of God, which passeth all understanding, shall keep your hearts and minds through Christ Jesus.

Key to Bind and Loose

Matthew 16:19

¹⁹ And I will give unto thee the keys of the kingdom of heaven: and whatsoever thou shalt bind on earth shall be bound in heaven: and whatsoever thou shalt loose on earth shall be loosed in heaven.

Ask and Receive

John 14:13

[13] And whatsoever ye shall ask in my name, that will I do, that the Father may be glorified in the Son.

Truth and Knowledge

Psalm 25:4

[4] Shew me thy ways, O LORD; teach me thy paths.

Ephesians 3:4

[4] Whereby, when ye read, ye may understand my knowledge in the mystery of Christ)

Healing

Mark 1:41

[41] And Jesus, moved with compassion, put forth [his] hand, and touched him, and saith unto him, I will; be thou clean.

Psalm 107:20

[20] He sent his word, and healed them, and delivered [them] from their destructions.

Luke 10:9

[9] And heal the sick that are therein, and say unto them, The kingdom of God is come nigh unto you.

Mark 16:18

<u>18 They shall take up serpents; and if they drink any deadly thing, it shall not hurt them; they shall lay hands on the sick, and they shall recover.</u>

Luke 4:18

<u>18 The Spirit of the Lord [is] upon me, because he hath anointed me to preach the gospel to the poor; he hath sent me to heal the brokenhearted, to preach deliverance to the captives, and recovering of sight to the blind, to set at liberty them that are bruised,</u>

Matthew 10:7-8

<u>7 And as ye go, preach, saying, The kingdom of heaven is at hand.</u>

<u>8 Heal the sick, cleanse the lepers, raise the dead, cast out devils: freely ye have received, freely give.</u>

Jeremiah 17:14

<u>14 Heal me, O LORD, and I shall be healed; save me, and I shall be saved: for thou [art] my praise.</u>

Psalm 103:2-3

<u>2 Bless the LORD, O my soul, and forget not all his benefits:</u>

<u>3 Who forgiveth all thine iniquities; who healeth all thy diseases;</u>

Defeating the enemy

Ephesians 6:11-12
11 Put on the whole armour of God, that ye may be able to stand against the wiles of the devil.
12 For we wrestle not against flesh and blood, but against principalities, against powers, against the rulers of the darkness of this world, against spiritual wickedness in high [places].

Luke 4:41
41 And devils also came out of many, crying out, and saying, Thou art Christ the Son of God. And he rebuking [them] suffered them not to speak: for they knew that he was Christ.

Malachi 4:3
3 And ye shall tread down the wicked; for they shall be ashes under the soles of your feet in the day that I shall do [this], saith the LORD of hosts.

Psalm 55:15-16
15 Let death seize upon them, [and] let them go down quick into hell: for wickedness [is] in their dwellings, [and] among them.
16 As for me, I will call upon God; and the LORD shall save me.

Roman 16:20

20 And the God of peace shall bruise Satan under your feet shortly. The grace of our Lord Jesus Christ [be] with you. Amen.

Luke 10:19

19 Behold, I give unto you power to tread on serpents and scorpions, and over all the power of the enemy: and nothing shall by any means hurt you.

2 Timothy 4:18

18 And the Lord shall deliver me from every evil work, and will preserve [me] unto his heavenly kingdom: to whom [be] glory for ever and ever. Amen.

Psalm 121:7

7 The LORD shall preserve thee from all evil: he shall preserve thy soul.

Proverb 28:1

1 The wicked flee when no man pursueth: but the righteous are bold as a lion.

James 4:7

7 Submit yourselves therefore to God. Resist the devil, and he will flee from you.

Exodus 14:14

14 The LORD shall fight for you, and ye shall hold your peace.

Colossians 2:15

¹⁵ [And] having spoiled principalities and powers, he made a shew of them openly, triumphing over them in it.

Luke 11:20

²⁰ But if I with the finger of God cast out devils, no doubt the kingdom of God is come upon you.

Holy Spirit

John 16:13

¹³ Howbeit when he, the Spirit of truth, is come, he will guide you into all truth: for he shall not speak of himself; but whatsoever he shall hear, [that] shall he speak: and he will shew you things to come.

Roman 8:11

¹¹ But if the Spirit of him that raised up Jesus from the dead dwell in you, he that raised up Christ from the dead shall also quicken your mortal bodies by his Spirit that dwelleth in you.

Roman 8:16

¹⁶ The Spirit itself beareth witness with our spirit, that we are the children of God:

Roman 8:26-27

²⁶ Likewise the Spirit also helpeth our infirmities: for we know not what we should pray for as we ought: but the Spirit itself maketh intercession for us with groanings which cannot be uttered.

²⁷ And he that searcheth the hearts knoweth what [is] the mind of the Spirit, because he maketh intercession for the saints according to [the will of] God.

1 Corinthians 2:10-13

¹⁰ But God hath revealed [them] unto us by his Spirit: for the Spirit searcheth all things, yea, the deep things of God.

¹¹ For what man knoweth the things of a man, save the spirit of man which is in him? even so the things of God knoweth no man, but the Spirit of God.

¹² Now we have received, not the spirit of the world, but the spirit which is of God; that we might know the things that are freely given to us of God.

¹³ Which things also we speak, not in the words which man's wisdom teacheth, but which the Holy Ghost teacheth; comparing spiritual things with spiritual.

Psalms

Psalm 1

¹ Blessed [is] the man that walketh not in the counsel of the ungodly, nor standeth in the way of sinners, nor sitteth in the seat of the scornful.

² But his delight [is] in the law of the LORD; and in his law doth he meditate day and night.

³ And he shall be like a tree planted by the rivers of water, that bringeth forth his fruit in his season; his leaf also shall not wither; and whatsoever he doeth shall prosper.

⁴ The ungodly [are] not so: but [are] like the chaff which the wind driveth away.

5 Therefore the ungodly shall not stand in the judgment, nor sinners in the congregation of the righteous.

6 For the LORD knoweth the way of the righteous: but the way of the ungodly shall perish.

Psalm 2

1 Why do the heathen rage, and the people imagine a vain thing?

2 The kings of the earth set themselves, and the rulers take counsel together, against the LORD, and against his anointed, [saying],

3 Let us break their bands asunder, and cast away their cords from us.

4 He that sitteth in the heavens shall laugh: the Lord shall have them in derision.

5 Then shall he speak unto them in his wrath, and vex them in his sore displeasure.

6 Yet have I set my king upon my holy hill of Zion.

7 I will declare the decree: the LORD hath said unto me, Thou [art] my Son; this day have I begotten thee.

8 Ask of me, and I shall give [thee] the heathen [for] thine inheritance, and the uttermost parts of the earth [for] thy possession.

9 Thou shalt break them with a rod of iron; thou shalt dash them in pieces like a potter's vessel.

10 Be wise now therefore, O ye kings: be instructed, ye judges of the earth.

11 Serve the LORD with fear, and rejoice with trembling.

12 Kiss the Son, lest he be angry, and ye perish [from] the way, when his wrath is kindled but a little. Blessed [are] all they that put their trust in him.

Psalm 3

1   (A Psalm of David, when he fled from Absalom his son.) LORD, how are they increased that trouble me! many [are] they that rise up against me.

2   Many [there be] which say of my soul, [There is] no help for him in God. Selah.

3   But thou, O LORD, [art] a shield for me; my glory, and the lifter up of mine head.

4   I cried unto the LORD with my voice, and he heard me out of his holy hill. Selah.

5   I laid me down and slept; I awaked; for the LORD sustained me.

6   I will not be afraid of ten thousands of people, that have set [themselves] against me round about.

7   Arise, O LORD; save me, O my God: for thou hast smitten all mine enemies [upon] the cheek bone; thou hast broken the teeth of the ungodly.

8   Salvation [belongeth] unto the LORD: thy blessing [is] upon thy people. Selah.

Psalm 4

1   (To the chief Musician on Neginoth, A Psalm of David.) Hear me when I call, O God of my righteousness: thou hast enlarged me [when I was] in distress; have mercy upon me, and hear my prayer.

2   O ye sons of men, how long [will ye turn] my glory into shame? [how long] will ye love vanity, [and] seek after leasing? Selah.

3   But know that the LORD hath set apart him that is godly for himself: the LORD will hear when I call unto him.

4 Stand in awe, and sin not: commune with your own heart upon your bed, and be still. Selah.

5 Offer the sacrifices of righteousness, and put your trust in the LORD.

6 [There be] many that say, Who will shew us [any] good? LORD, lift thou up the light of thy countenance upon us.

7 Thou hast put gladness in my heart, more than in the time [that] their corn and their wine increased.

8 I will both lay me down in peace, and sleep: for thou, LORD, only makest me dwell in safety.

Psalm 5

1 (To the chief Musician upon Nehiloth, A Psalm of David.) Give ear to my words, O LORD, consider my meditation.

2 Hearken unto the voice of my cry, my King, and my God: for unto thee will I pray.

3 My voice shalt thou hear in the morning, O LORD; in the morning will I direct [my prayer] unto thee, and will look up.

4 For thou [art] not a God that hath pleasure in wickedness: neither shall evil dwell with thee.

5 The foolish shall not stand in thy sight: thou hatest all workers of iniquity.

6 Thou shalt destroy them that speak leasing: the LORD will abhor the bloody and deceitful man.

7 But as for me, I will come [into] thy house in the multitude of thy mercy: [and] in thy fear will I worship toward thy holy temple.

8 Lead me, O LORD, in thy righteousness because of mine enemies; make thy way straight before my face.

9 For [there is] no faithfulness in their mouth; their inward part [is] very wickedness; their throat [is] an open sepulchre; they flatter with their tongue.

10 Destroy thou them, O God; let them fall by their own counsels; cast them out in the multitude of their transgressions; for they have rebelled against thee.

11 But let all those that put their trust in thee rejoice: let them ever shout for joy, because thou defendest them: let them also that love thy name be joyful in thee.

12 For thou, LORD, wilt bless the righteous; with favour wilt thou compass him as [with] a shield.

Psalm 6

1 (To the chief Musician on Neginoth upon Sheminith, A Psalm of David.) O LORD, rebuke me not in thine anger, neither chasten me in thy hot displeasure.

2 Have mercy upon me, O LORD; for I [am] weak: O LORD, heal me; for my bones are vexed.

3 My soul is also sore vexed: but thou, O LORD, how long?

4 Return, O LORD, deliver my soul: oh save me for thy mercies' sake.

5 For in death [there is] no remembrance of thee: in the grave who shall give thee thanks?

6 I am weary with my groaning; all the night make I my bed to swim; I water my couch with my tears.

7 Mine eye is consumed because of grief; it waxeth old because of all mine enemies.

8 Depart from me, all ye workers of iniquity; for the LORD hath heard the voice of my weeping.

9 The LORD hath heard my supplication; the LORD will receive my prayer.

10 Let all mine enemies be ashamed and sore vexed: let them return [and] be ashamed suddenly.

Psalm 7

1 (Shiggaion of David, which he sang unto the LORD, concerning the words of Cush the Benjamite.) O LORD my God, in thee do I put my trust: save me from all them that persecute me, and deliver me:

2 Lest he tear my soul like a lion, rending [it] in pieces, while [there is] none to deliver.

3 O LORD my God, if I have done this; if there be iniquity in my hands;

4 If I have rewarded evil unto him that was at peace with me; (yea, I have delivered him that without cause is mine enemy:)

5 Let the enemy persecute my soul, and take [it]; yea, let him tread down my life upon the earth, and lay mine honour in the dust. Selah.

6 Arise, O LORD, in thine anger, lift up thyself because of the rage of mine enemies: and awake for me [to] the judgment [that] thou hast commanded.

7 So shall the congregation of the people compass thee about: for their sakes therefore return thou on high.

8 The LORD shall judge the people: judge me, O LORD, according to my righteousness, and according to mine integrity [that is] in me.

9 Oh let the wickedness of the wicked come to an end; but establish the just: for the righteous God trieth the hearts and reins.

10 My defence [is] of God, which saveth the upright in heart.

11 God judgeth the righteous, and God is angry [with the wicked] every day.

12 If he turn not, he will whet his sword; he hath bent his bow, and made it ready.

13 He hath also prepared for him the instruments of death; he ordaineth his arrows against the persecutors.

14 Behold, he travaileth with iniquity, and hath conceived mischief, and brought forth falsehood.

15 He made a pit, and digged it, and is fallen into the ditch [which] he made.

16 His mischief shall return upon his own head, and his violent dealing shall come down upon his own pate.

17 I will praise the LORD according to his righteousness: and will sing praise to the name of the LORD most high.

Psalm 8

1 (To the chief Musician upon Gittith, A Psalm of David.) O LORD our Lord, how excellent [is] thy name in all the earth! who hast set thy glory above the heavens.

2 Out of the mouth of babes and sucklings hast thou ordained strength because of thine enemies, that thou mightest still the enemy and the avenger.

3 When I consider thy heavens, the work of thy fingers, the moon and the stars, which thou hast ordained;

4 What is man, that thou art mindful of him? and the son
   of man, that thou visitest him?

5 For thou hast made him a little lower than the angels,
   and hast crowned him with glory and honour.

6 Thou madest him to have dominion over the works of
   thy hands; thou hast put all [things] under his feet:

7 All sheep and oxen, yea, and the beasts of the field;

8 The fowl of the air, and the fish of the sea, [and
   whatsoever] passeth through the paths of the seas.

9 O LORD our Lord, how excellent [is] thy name in all
   the earth!

Psalm 91

1 He that dwelleth in the secret place of the most High
   shall abide under the shadow of the Almighty.

2 I will say of the LORD, [He is] my refuge and my fortress:
   my God; in him will I trust.

3 Surely he shall deliver thee from the snare of the fowler,
   [and] from the noisome pestilence.

4 He shall cover thee with his feathers, and under his
   wings shalt thou trust: his truth [shall be thy] shield and
   buckler.

5 Thou shalt not be afraid for the terror by night; [nor] for
   the arrow [that] flieth by day;

6 [Nor] for the pestilence [that] walketh in darkness; [nor]
   for the destruction [that] wasteth at noonday.

7 A thousand shall fall at thy side, and ten thousand at thy
   right hand; [but] it shall not come nigh thee.

8 Only with thine eyes shalt thou behold and see the
   reward of the wicked.

9   Because thou hast made the LORD, [which is] my refuge, [even] the most High, thy habitation;

10 There shall no evil befall thee, neither shall any plague come nigh thy dwelling.

11 For he shall give his angels charge over thee, to keep thee in all thy ways.

12 They shall bear thee up in [their] hands, lest thou dash thy foot against a stone.

13 Thou shalt tread upon the lion and adder: the young lion and the dragon shalt thou trample under feet.

14 Because he hath set his love upon me, therefore will I deliver him: I will set him on high, because he hath known my name.

15 He shall call upon me, and I will answer him: I [will be] with him in trouble; I will deliver him, and honour him.

16 With long life will I satisfy him, and shew him my salvation.

Psalm 109

1 (To the chief Musician, A Psalm of David.) Hold not thy peace, O God of my praise;

2 For the mouth of the wicked and the mouth of the deceitful are opened against me: they have spoken against me with a lying tongue.

3 They compassed me about also with words of hatred; and fought against me without a cause.

4 For my love they are my adversaries: but I [give myself unto] prayer.

5 And they have rewarded me evil for good, and hatred for my love.

⁶ Set thou a wicked man over him: and let Satan stand at his right hand.

⁷ When he shall be judged, let him be condemned: and let his prayer become sin.

⁸ Let his days be few; [and] let another take his office.

⁹ Let his children be fatherless, and his wife a widow.

¹⁰ Let his children be continually vagabonds, and beg: let them seek [their bread] also out of their desolate places.

¹¹ Let the extortioner catch all that he hath; and let the strangers spoil his labour.

¹² Let there be none to extend mercy unto him: neither let there be any to favour his fatherless children.

¹³ Let his posterity be cut off; [and] in the generation following let their name be blotted out.

¹⁴ Let the iniquity of his fathers be remembered with the LORD; and let not the sin of his mother be blotted out.

¹⁵ Let them be before the LORD continually, that he may cut off the memory of them from the earth.

¹⁶ Because that he remembered not to shew mercy, but persecuted the poor and needy man, that he might even slay the broken in heart.

¹⁷ As he loved cursing, so let it come unto him: as he delighted not in blessing, so let it be far from him.

¹⁸ As he clothed himself with cursing like as with his garment, so let it come into his bowels like water, and like oil into his bones.

¹⁹ Let it be unto him as the garment [which] covereth him, and for a girdle wherewith he is girded continually.

²⁰ [Let] this [be] the reward of mine adversaries from the LORD, and of them that speak evil against my soul.

21 But do thou for me, O GOD the Lord, for thy name's sake: because thy mercy [is] good, deliver thou me.

22 For I [am] poor and needy, and my heart is wounded within me.

23 I am gone like the shadow when it declineth: I am tossed up and down as the locust.

24 My knees are weak through fasting; and my flesh faileth of fatness.

25 I became also a reproach unto them: [when] they looked upon me they shaked their heads.

26 Help me, O LORD my God: O save me according to thy mercy:

27 That they may know that this [is] thy hand; [that] thou, LORD, hast done it.

28 Let them curse, but bless thou: when they arise, let them be ashamed; but let thy servant rejoice.

29 Let mine adversaries be clothed with shame, and let them cover themselves with their own confusion, as with a mantle.

30 I will greatly praise the LORD with my mouth; yea, I will praise him among the multitude.

31 For he shall stand at the right hand of the poor, to save [him] from those that condemn his soul.

Psalm 116

1 I love the LORD, because he hath heard my voice [and] my supplications.

2 Because he hath inclined his ear unto me, therefore will I call upon [him] as long as I live.

3 The sorrows of death compassed me, and the pains of hell gat hold upon me: I found trouble and sorrow.

⁴ Then called I upon the name of the LORD; O LORD, I beseech thee, deliver my soul.

⁵ Gracious [is] the LORD, and righteous; yea, our God [is] merciful.

⁶ The LORD preserveth the simple: I was brought low, and he helped me.

⁷ Return unto thy rest, O my soul; for the LORD hath dealt bountifully with thee.

⁸ For thou hast delivered my soul from death, mine eyes from tears, [and] my feet from falling.

⁹ I will walk before the LORD in the land of the living.

¹⁰ I believed, therefore have I spoken: I was greatly afflicted:

¹¹ I said in my haste, All men [are] liars.

¹² What shall I render unto the LORD [for] all his benefits toward me?

¹³ I will take the cup of salvation, and call upon the name of the LORD.

¹⁴ I will pay my vows unto the LORD now in the presence of all his people.

¹⁵ Precious in the sight of the LORD [is] the death of his saints.

¹⁶ O LORD, truly I [am] thy servant; I [am] thy servant, [and] the son of thine handmaid: thou hast loosed my bonds.

¹⁷ I will offer to thee the sacrifice of thanksgiving, and will call upon the name of the LORD.

¹⁸ I will pay my vows unto the LORD now in the presence of all his people,

¹⁹ In the courts of the LORD'S house, in the midst of thee, O Jerusalem. Praise ye the LORD.

And devils also came out of many crying out and saying "Thou art CHRIST SON OF GOD and he rebuking them suffered them not to speak for they knew he was CHRIST.

Luke 4:41